CUBAN COOKBOOK 2021

DISCOVER THE TRUE FLAVORS OF CUBA WITH THE BEST AND ORIGINAL CUBAN RECIPES

THE PICADILLO PRESS

The Picadillo Press

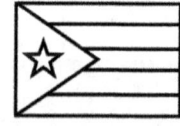

TABLE OF CONTENTS:

CHAPTER 1: CUBAN RECIPES 6

- CUBAN MINI MELTS 7
- CUBAN-STYLE PICADILLO 9
- CUBAN GRILLED CHICKEN SALAD 11
- AMAZING SHREDDED SLOW COOKER CUBAN BEEF 13
- CUBAN SLIDERS 15
- SLOW COOKER CUBAN PORK 18
- RABO ENCENDIDO 20
- CUBAN CHICKEN SANDWICH 23
- PESCADO CON QUESO 26
- CUBAN SANDWICH BITES 28
- CUBAN BREAD 30
- CUBAN BANANA CASSEROLE 34
- CUBAN-STYLE SLOW-COOKER CHICKEN FRICASSEE 36
- PACIFIC CUBAN BLACK BEANS AND RICE 38
- CUBAN SHREDDED PORK 41
- ROPA VIEJA 43
- MIAMI CUBAN DIP 47
- CUBAN PORK ROAST 50
- CUBAN SMOKED SAUSAGE WITH CHICKPEAS 53
- CUBAN BEANS AND RICE 55
- CUBAN BLACK BEANS 57
- CLASSIC CUBAN MIDNIGHT 59
- CUBAN GOULASH 61
- CUBAN GREEN SOUP 63
- AMAZING CUBAN TAMALES 65
- TAMPA CUBAN HAND PIES 69
- CUBAN-STYLE YELLOW RICE 72
- GRILLED TURKEY CUBAN SANDWICHES 74
- CUBAN MARINATED STEAK 77
- FRITAS CUBANAS 80
- RABBIT FRICASSEE CUBAN-STYLE 82
- CUBAN-STYLE MOJO SHRIMP 84
- SEA BASS CUBAN STYLE 87
- AMAZING LOMO DE RES, CUBAN-STYLE RIB-EYE STEAKS 89

BAKED CUBAN CHICKEN	92
CUBAN-STYLE PORK AND SWEET POTATOES	95
CHICKEN FRIED STEAK CUBAN STYLE	97
TURKEY PICADILLO	99
SPICY CUBAN MOJO CHICKEN WITH MANGO-AVOCADO SALSA	101
CUBAN BEEF AND ZUCCHINI KEBABS WITH MOJO SAUCE	104
CARNE CON PAPAS	107
ARROZ CON LECHE	109

© Copyright 2021 by The Picadillo Press All rights reserved.

The following Book is reproduced below with the goal of providing information that is as accurate and reliable as possible. Regardless, purchasing this Book can be seen as consent to the fact that both the publisher and the author of this book are in no way experts on the topics discussed within and that any recommendations or suggestions that are made herein are for entertainment purposes only.

Professionals should

be consulted as

needed prior to undertaking any of the action endorsed herein.

This declaration is deemed fair and valid by both the American Bar Association and the Committee of Publishers Association and is legally binding throughout the United States.

Furthermore, the transmission, duplication, or reproduction of any of the following work including specific information will be considered an illegal act irrespective of if it is done electronically or in print. This extends to creating a secondary or tertiary copy of the work or a recorded copy and is only allowed with the express written consent from the Publisher. All additional right reserved.

The information in the following pages is broadly considered a truthful and accurate account of facts and as such, any inattention, use, or misuse of the information in question by the reader will render any resulting actions solely under their purview. There are no scenarios in which the publisher or the original author of this work can be in any fashion deemed liable for any hardship or damages that may befall them after undertaking information described herein.

Additionally, the information in the following pages

is intended only for informational purposes and should thus

be thought of as universal. As befitting its nature,

it is presented without assurance

regarding its prolonged validity or interim quality. Trademarks that are mentioned are done without written consent and can in no way be considered an endorsement from the trademark holder.

CHAPTER 1: CUBAN RECIPES

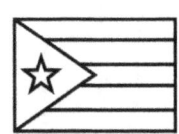

CUBAN MINI MELTS

Prep:
15 mins
Cook:
10 mins
Total:
25 mins
Servings:
10
Yield:
20 mini sandwiches

INGREDIENTS:

10 slices white sandwich bread, quartered
12 slices honey ham, chopped
1 ½ cups shredded Swiss cheese
2 tablespoons spicy brown mustard
2 tablespoons mayonnaise
20 dill pickle slices
20 toothpicks

DIRECTIONS:

1

Preheat the oven to 450 degrees F (230 degrees C). Divide quartered bread slices evenly between 2 large baking sheets.

2

Combine ham, Swiss cheese, mustard, and mayonnaise in a large bowl and mix well. Place 1 tablespoon of mixture on top of each piece of bread on 1 of the baking sheets.

3

Bake topped bread in the preheated oven for 4 minutes. Add baking sheet with plain bread to the oven and continue baking 3 minutes more.

4

Remove both baking sheets from the oven. Place a dill pickle slice on each topped bread slice; cover with a piece of plain toasted bread. Secure each mini sandwich with a toothpick.

NUTRITION FACTS:

208 calories; protein 12.1g; carbohydrates 15.6g; fat 10.6g; cholesterol 35.1mg; sodium 873.5mg.

CUBAN-STYLE PICADILLO

Prep:
10 mins
Cook:
20 mins
Total:
30 mins
Servings:
4
Yield:
4 servings

INGREDIENTS:

- 1 tablespoon olive oil
- 1 clove garlic, minced, or more to taste
- 1 small onion, chopped
- ½ green bell pepper, chopped
- 1 pound lean ground beef
- 6 large pitted green olives, quartered
- ½ cup raisins
- 1 tablespoon capers (Optional)
- 1 (8 ounce) can tomato sauce
- 2 (1.41 ounce) packages sazon seasoning
- 1 tablespoon ground cumin

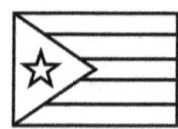

1 teaspoon white sugar

salt to taste

DIRECTIONS:

1

Heat olive oil in a skillet over medium heat; cook and stir garlic, onion, and green bell pepper in the hot oil until softened, 5 to 7 minutes.

2

Crumble ground beef into the skillet; cook and stir until browned completely, 7 to 10 minutes.

3

Stir olives, raisins, capers, tomato sauce, sazon seasoning, cumin, sugar, and salt through the ground beef mixture.

4

Cover the skillet, reduce heat to low, and cook until the mixture is heated through, 5 to 10 minutes.

NUTRITION FACTS:

350 calories; protein 23.7g; carbohydrates 23.8g; fat 18.5g; cholesterol 74.3mg; sodium 3571.8mg

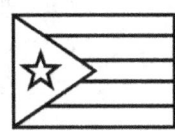

CUBAN GRILLED CHICKEN SALAD

Prep:
15 mins
Total:
15 mins
Servings:
4
Yield:
4 servings

INGREDIENTS:

3 cups chopped romaine lettuce
1 small red onion, diced
1 (6 ounce) avocado, diced
½ cup red or yellow bell pepper, diced
¾ cup canned black beans, drained
¾ cup diced fresh or canned pineapple
2 cups cooked chicken meat, chopped
2 tablespoons olive oil
2 teaspoons minced garlic
salt and pepper to taste
4 teaspoons fresh lime juice

DIRECTIONS:

1

Toss the romaine with the onion, avocado, and peppers in a large bowl. Divide among four salad plates. Top each salad with a mound of black beans, some pineapple chunks, and the chopped chicken meat.

2

Whisk together the olive oil with the garlic, salt, and pepper. Drizzle this dressing over each salad along with a little lime juice.

NUTRITION FACTS:

292 calories; protein 17.6g; carbohydrates 25.6g; fat 14.8g; cholesterol 34.3mg;

AMAZING SHREDDED SLOW COOKER CUBAN BEEF

Prep:
30 mins
Cook:
7 hrs 10 mins
Total:
7 hrs 40 mins
Servings:
4
Yield:
4 servings

INGREDIENTS:

1 pound rump roast
coarse salt to taste
ground black pepper to taste
1 tablespoon olive oil
¾ cup bitter orange marinade
¾ cup garlic marinade
1 yellow onion, sliced
4 large cloves garlic, minced, or more to taste
½ tablespoon ground cumin

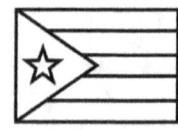

DIRECTIONS:

1

Cut roast into 4 quarters and season liberally with salt and pepper. Place a large cast iron pan over high heat and coat with olive oil; heat until smoking. Place meat in the hot pan and turn to sear on all sides until a crust forms, 5 to 10 minutes. Transfer seared meat to a slow cooker.

2

Add bitter orange marinade, garlic marinade, onion, garlic, and cumin to the slow cooker. Make sure meat is mostly covered in marinade.

3

Cook on Low for 6 hours; shred meat in the slow cooker using tongs or a fork. Continue cooking on Low for another 1 to 1 1/2 hours. Add additional salt or cumin if desired.

NUTRITION FACTS:

258 calories; protein 21g; carbohydrates 16g; fat 11.6g; cholesterol 50mg; sodium 798.5mg.

CUBAN SLIDERS

Prep:
20 mins
Cook:
35 mins
Additional:
20 mins
Total:
75 mins
Servings:
24
Yield:
24 servings

INGREDIENTS:

2 (12 count) packages Hawaiian bread rolls
½ cup butter, melted
2 tablespoons Dijon mustard
Worcestershire sauce
1 tablespoon onion powder
1 tablespoon poppy seeds
1 pound cooked pulled pork without sauce
24 slices honey-cured deli ham
½ pound sliced Swiss cheese, or more as needed
48 dill pickle chips, patted dry

DIRECTIONS:

1

Grease bottom and sides of a 9x13-inch baking dish or disposable aluminum pan.

2

Cut Hawaiian rolls in half. Arrange 24 bottom halves in the baking dish.

3

Mix melted butter, Dijon mustard, Worcestershire sauce, onion powder, and poppy seeds together in a bowl. Brush 1/2 half the butter mixture over the bottom halves in the baking dish.

4

Layer pulled pork, ham, Swiss cheese, and 2 pickle chips to each roll, in this order, and cover with tops of rolls. Brush remaining butter mixture over the tops. Cover with aluminum foil and refrigerate for 20 to 30 minutes.

5

Preheat oven to 350 degrees F (175 degrees C).

6

Bake sliders in the preheated oven, covered, for 20 minutes. Remove foil and press down the tops of the sliders with a spatula to flatten. Bake until sliders are heated through and top is crispy, about 15 minutes more.

NUTRITION FACTS:

398 calories; protein 23.6g; carbohydrates 45.8g; fat 8g; cholesterol 80mg; sodium 651.4mg.

SLOW COOKER CUBAN PORK

Prep:
30 mins
Cook:
9 hrs
Additional:
1 hr
Total:
10 hrs 30 mins
Servings:
12

INGREDIENTS:

1 (5 pound) boneless pork loin, trimmed and silver skin removed
1 cup orange juice (such as Simply®)
½ cup lime juice
½ cup lemon juice
14 whole black peppercorns
1 large onion, finely chopped
1 head garlic, peeled and pressed
2 tablespoons kosher salt
1 teaspoon kosher salt
1 tablespoon dried oregano

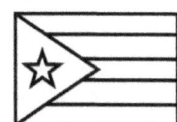

DIRECTIONS:

1

Cut pork loin into 3 equal pieces.

2

Turn a slow cooker to Low. Add orange juice, lime juice, lemon juice, and peppercorns, then add onion.

3

Mix garlic, salt, and oregano into a paste and rub all over pork pieces. Place pork in the slow cooker.

4

Cook on Low until pork is slightly pink in the center, 9 to 10 hours. An instant-read thermometer inserted into the center should read at least 145 degrees F (63 degrees C). Pull apart meat with 2 forks and let sit for 1 hour before serving.

NUTRITION FACTS:

298 calories; protein 31.3g; carbohydrates 7.6g; fat 15.4g; cholesterol 89.6mg; sodium 1176.1mg.

RABO ENCENDIDO

Prep:
35 mins
Cook:
4 hrs 14 mins
Additional:
12 hrs
Total:
16 hrs 49 mins
Servings:
8
Yield:
8 servings

INGREDIENTS:

- 1 ½ cups vino seco (white cooking wine)
- ¼ cup olive oil
- 1 teaspoon salt
- 4 pounds beef oxtails
- 2 tablespoons olive oil, divided
- 2 potatoes, peeled and quartered
- 2 cups diced onion
- 1 cup diced carrots
- 6 cloves garlic, coarsely chopped
- ½ teaspoon salt
- ¼ cup green olives, pitted and halved

3 bay leaves
2 teaspoons Miami-style sazon seasoning (sazon completa)
½ (.18 ounce) packet sazon seasoning (such as Sa-Son Accent®)
½ teaspoon allspice
2 (15 ounce) cans tomato sauce
3 cups chicken broth

DIRECTIONS:

1
Whisk vino seco, 1/4 cup olive oil, and salt together in a large bowl. Add oxtails and mix well to coat. Cover with plastic wrap and marinate in the refrigerator for 12 hours.

2
Drain oxtails, discarding all but 1/2 cup of the marinade.

3
Heat 1 tablespoon olive oil in a large pot over medium-high heat and sear oxtails until browned on all sides, about 2 minutes per side. Transfer to a large plate. Heat remaining 1 tablespoon olive oil in the same pot. Saute potatoes, onion, and carrots until onions are translucent, about 5 minutes.

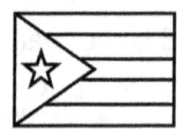

4

Mash garlic and 1/2 teaspoon salt into a coarse paste in a mortar and pestle. Add garlic paste to the pot; stir until fragrant, about 30 seconds. Stir in green olives, bay leaves, sazon completa, sazon seasoning, and allspice. Pour in reserved marinade, tomato sauce, and chicken broth.

5

Return oxtails to the pot. Bring to a boil, reduce heat, and simmer, covered, until oxtails are fork tender and falling off the bone, about 4 hours.

NUTRITION FACTS:

785 calories; protein 72.9g; carbohydrates 23g; fat 41.8g; cholesterol 251.6mg; sodium 2008.4mg.

CUBAN CHICKEN SANDWICH

Prep:
15 mins
Cook:
10 mins
Additional:
2 hrs
Total:
2 hrs 25 mins
Servings:
4
Yield:
4 sandwiches

INGREDIENTS:

1 ½ pounds chicken tenders
½ cup mojo marinade, or as needed
1 tablespoon olive oil, or more as needed
8 thin slices sweet onion
1 (1 pound) loaf Cuban bread
¼ cup yellow mustard
20 dill pickle slices
4 slices Swiss cheese

DIRECTIONS:

1

Place chicken tenders between 2 sheets of heavy plastic on a solid, level surface. Firmly pound chicken with the smooth side of a meat mallet until flattened out. Place chicken in a resealable plastic bag and add enough mojo marinade to cover the chicken. Marinate in the refrigerator for 2 hours, or up to overnight.

2

Heat olive oil in a large skillet over medium heat. Remove chicken tenders from the marinade, drain, and place in the skillet. Cook until lightly browned, 2 to 3 minutes per side. An instant-read thermometer inserted into the center should read at least 165 degrees F (74 degrees C). Transfer chicken to a plate.

3

Add sliced onions to the same skillet, adding a bit more oil if necessary, and cook until softened, about 3 minutes. Remove from skillet.

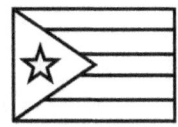

4

Cut Cuban bread into 4 rolls. Slice each in half lengthwise without cutting all the way through. Cover the bottom and the top of each roll with yellow mustard. Assemble the sandwich by placing pickle slices on the bottom, followed by chicken, Swiss cheese, and onion. Cut each sandwich in half at an angle, and serve.

NUTRITION FACTS:

661 calories; protein 54.1g; carbohydrates 64.4g; fat 19.4g;

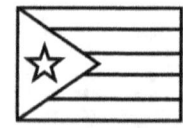

PESCADO CON QUESO

Prep:
10 mins
Cook:
45 mins
Total:
55 mins
Servings:
6
Yield:
6 servings

INGREDIENTS:

1 onion, chopped
½ pound shredded Cheddar cheese
2 pounds swai fish
1 teaspoon butter
1 cup milk
1½ teaspoons Worcestershire sauce
1 teaspoon mustard
1 teaspoon salt
ground black pepper to taste

DIRECTIONS:

1

Preheat oven to 350 degrees F (175 degrees C). Grease a 9x13-inch baking dish.

2

Mix onion and Cheddar cheese together in a bowl. Sprinkle 1/2 of the cheese mixture into the prepared baking dish; top with swai fish. Sprinkle the remaining cheese mixture over fish.

3

Whisk milk, Worcestershire sauce, mustard, salt, and black pepper together in a bowl; pour over fish.

4

Bake in the preheated oven until fish flakes easily with a fork and the cheese is melted, about 45 minutes.

NUTRITION FACTS:

376 calories; protein 33.4g; carbohydrates 6.4g; fat 23.6g; cholesterol 120.4mg; sodium 763.7mg.

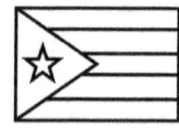

CUBAN SANDWICH BITES

Prep:
10 mins
Cook:
30 mins
Total:
40 mins
Servings:
24
Yield:
24 bites

INGREDIENTS:

1 baguette, cut into 1/2-inch slices
3 tablespoons yellow mustard
3 tablespoons Dijon mustard
1½ pounds Swiss cheese, sliced, divided
4 ounces dill pickle slices
1 pound honey ham, sliced
1 pound cooked pork loin, sliced
¼ cup mayonnaise
¼ teaspoon garlic powder
cooking spray

DIRECTIONS:

1

Preheat the oven to 350 degrees F (175 degrees C). Place a cooling rack on a rimmed baking sheet.

2

Mix yellow and Dijon mustards together and spread evenly over baguette slices. Top 1/2 of the bread slices with 1/2 of the Swiss cheese and place on the rack on the baking sheet. Top each with pickle slices, ham, pork loin, and remaining cheese. Top sandwiches with remaining baguette slices.

3

Spread mayonnaise over the tops of the sandwiches and sprinkle with garlic powder. Spray the bottom of a second baking pan with cooking spray and place upside-down on top of the sandwiches. Weigh down the top pan with a heavy, oven-safe item such as a cast iron skillet.

4

Bake in the preheated oven for 25 minutes. Remove top pan and bake until golden brown, about 5 minutes more.

NUTRITION FACTS:

241 calories; protein 15.9g; carbohydrates 10.3g; fat 15g;

CUBAN BREAD

Prep:
25 mins
Cook:
20 mins
Additional:
11 hrs 30 mins
Total:
11 hrs 75 mins
Servings:
12
Yield:
2 loaves

INGREDIENTS:

STARTER:

½ teaspoon active dry yeast
½ cup warm water
½ cup flour

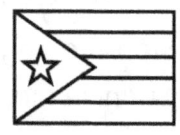

DOUGH:

1 package active dry yeast
2 teaspoons white sugar
¾ cup warm water
3 tablespoons lard
2 teaspoons fine salt
3 cups all-purpose flour, or as needed - divided
1 tablespoon cornmeal
Water to spray tops of loaves

DIRECTIONS:

1

Combine 1/2 cup warm water, 1/2 teaspoon yeast, and 1/2 cup flour in a bowl or measuring cup. Whisk the starter until well blended. Cover with plastic wrap and refrigerate overnight.

2

Place 1 package active dry yeast and 2 teaspoons sugar in a mixing bowl. Pour in 3/4 cup warm water. Let rest 15 minutes to ensure yeast is alive (bubbles will form on surface). Add lard and salt to bowl; add 1 cup of the flour. Mix until all ingredients are incorporated and dough forms a sticky ball. Add the starter (reserving 1/4 cup if you want to keep the starter going, if desired. Otherwise add it all.).
Sprinkle most of the rest of the flour on the dough, reserving 1/2 cup to be used if needed when kneading.

3

Turn dough out onto a lightly floured work surface and knead until dough comes together in a firm ball, adding additional flour only as needed. Dough should be soft and supple with just a bit of tackiness on the surface.

4

Place dough in a bowl and coat surface with a little vegetable oil. Cover bowl with a damp kitchen towel and place in a warm spot to rise. Let rise until at least doubled in size, about 2 hours.

5

Line two rimmed baking sheets with parchment paper and sprinkle with a little cornmeal.

6

Transfer dough onto lightly floured surface. Lightly press the dough into a rectangle with your lightly floured hands. Divide dough in half and press and shape each half into a long 1/2-inch thick rectangle about 12 inches long. Roll up tightly starting at the long end to form a skinny loaf. Flatten a bit. Transfer each loaf to a prepared baking sheet and dust with a bit of flour. Cover with a light, dry towel and let rise until doubled in size, 1 1/2 to 2 hours.

7

Preheat oven to 400 degrees F (200 degrees C). Cut a 1/4-inch deep slit down the top of the loaves with a sharp knife or razor. Mist loaves lightly with water.

8

Place pans in pre-heated oven, one pan on lower rack, one on higher rack. After 10 minutes, switch pan positions. Continue to bake until loaves are golden brown, 10 to 15 minutes longer. Transfer loaves to cooling rack and let cool to room temperature before slicing.

NUTRITION FACTS:

169 calories; protein 4.1g; carbohydrates 29.4g; fat 3.6g; cholesterol 3mg; sodium 389.5mg.

CUBAN BANANA CASSEROLE

Prep:
10 mins
Cook:
30 mins
Additional:
5 mins
Total:
45 mins
Servings:
8
Yield:
8 servings

INGREDIENTS:

6 bananas, sliced lengthwise
½ cup light brown sugar
½ cup unsalted butter, cut into small pieces
½ cup chopped pecans
½ cup raisins
1 tablespoon brandy

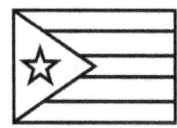

DIRECTIONS:

1

Preheat oven to 350 degrees F (175 degrees C). Lightly butter a 9x13 inch casserole dish.

2

Cover the bottom of the prepared casserole dish with half of the banana slices. Sprinkle the bananas with half the brown sugar, butter pieces, pecans, and raisins. Form another layer with the remaining banana slices and repeat layering with remaining brown sugar, butter, pecans, and raisins.

3

Bake in preheated oven for 30 minutes; remove from oven and cool for 5 minutes. Sprinkle brandy over top of dish to serve.

NUTRITION FACTS:

312 calories; protein 2g; carbohydrates 41.8g; fat 16.7g; cholesterol 30.5mg; sodium 7.3mg.

CUBAN-STYLE SLOW-COOKER CHICKEN FRICASSEE

Prep:
15 mins
Cook:
8 hrs
Total:
8 hrs 15 mins
Servings:
8

INGREDIENTS:

1 large onion, chopped
6 cloves garlic, chopped
½ green bell pepper, chopped
8 small whole peeled potatoes
1 (8 ounce) can tomato sauce
½ cup dry white wine
½ tablespoon cumin
1 leaf fresh sage
salt and pepper to taste
2 pounds chicken leg quarters

DIRECTIONS:

1

In a medium bowl, combine onion, garlic, bell pepper, and potatoes. Stir in tomato sauce and wine; season with cumin, sage leaf, and salt and pepper. Place chicken legs in slow cooker, and pour mixture over chicken. Cover, and cook on Low heat until juices run clear, about 6 to 8 hours.

NUTRITION FACTS:

316 calories; protein 23.3g; carbohydrates 21g; fat 14g; cholesterol 94.2mg; sodium 264.1mg.

PACIFIC CUBAN BLACK BEANS AND RICE

Prep:
20 mins
Cook:
1 hr 15 mins
Total:
1 hr 35 mins
Servings:
6
Yield:
6 servings

INGREDIENTS:

4 cups water
2 cups rice
3 tablespoons olive oil
1 onion, chopped
1 bell pepper, chopped
2 carrots, peeled and chopped
2 ribs celery, chopped
1 tablespoon minced garlic
2 (15 ounce) cans black beans

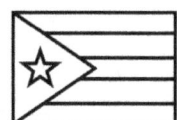

2 smoked Spanish chorizo sausage links, coarsely chopped
1 cup chicken stock
1 (8 ounce) jar picante sauce
2 bay leaves
2 teaspoons smoked paprika
1 teaspoon red wine vinegar, or more to taste
1 teaspoon ground cumin
1 teaspoon white sugar
1 teaspoon salt, or to taste
½ teaspoon ground black pepper, or to taste
1 pinch red pepper flakes (Optional)

DIRECTIONS:

1

Bring water and rice to a boil in a saucepan. Reduce heat to medium-low, cover, and simmer until the rice is tender and liquid has been absorbed, 20 to 25 minutes.

2

Heat olive oil in a stockpot over medium-high heat; saute onion, bell pepper, carrots, celery, and garlic in hot oil until tender, about 5 minutes.

3

Mix black beans with liquid, chorizo, chicken stock, picante sauce, bay leaves, paprika, red wine vinegar, cumin, sugar, salt, black pepper, and red pepper flakes together in the pot with the onion mixture; bring to a boil, reduce heat to medium-low, place a cover on the pot, and simmer until the beans have softened, about 30 minutes.

4

Remove lid from pot and continue cooking until the mixture reaches your desired consistency, at least 20 minutes more. Remove bay leaves and adjust seasoning to your preferences. Serve over rice.

NUTRITION FACTS:

559 calories; protein 19.6g; carbohydrates 84.5g; fat 15.8g; cholesterol 18.4mg; sodium 1609mg

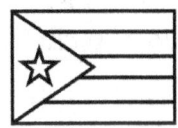

CUBAN SHREDDED PORK

Prep:
1 hr 30 mins
Cook:
15 mins
Total:
1 hr 45 mins

INGREDIENTS:

1½ pounds boneless pork chops
1 pint water to cover
1 lime, juiced
1 sprig fresh thyme
8 black peppercorns
1 tablespoon garlic powder, or to taste
1 tablespoon onion powder
salt to taste
2 tablespoons olive oil
1 large onion, halved and thinly sliced
3 cloves garlic, peeled and sliced
1 lime, juiced
¼ cup chopped fresh cilantro

DIRECTIONS:

1

In a large saucepan, combine water, juice of one lime, thyme sprig, peppercorns, garlic powder, onion powder and salt. Bring mixture to a boil. Add pork chops, reduce heat to medium-low and simmer for 1 to 1 1/2 hours, until meat is very tender. Add more water as necessary to keep chops covered.

2

Turn off heat and let the chops rest in the broth for 30 minutes. Remove chops from broth and shred, removing excess fat; set aside.

3

In a large frying pan, heat olive oil over medium-high heat. Add the shredded pork and fry until it is almost crisp, about 5 minutes. Add the onion and garlic and continue to cook until the onion is just tender yet slightly crisp, about 10 minutes more. Add the juice of one lime, mix though and toss with cilantro. Serve and enjoy.

NUTRITION FACTS:

202 calories; protein 18.5g; carbohydrates 8.1g; fat 10.7g; cholesterol 43.4mg; sodium 103.2mg.

ROPA VIEJA

Prep:
15 mins
Cook:
2 hrs 30 mins
Additional:
8 hrs 45 mins
Total:
10 hrs 90 mins
Servings:
8
Yield:
8 servings

INGREDIENTS:

1 (1 1/2-pound) flank steak
2 teaspoons kosher salt, or more to taste
1 teaspoon freshly ground black pepper
1 pinch cayenne pepper, or to taste
2 tablespoons olive oil
1 large red onion, sliced
4 cloves garlic, sliced
2 teaspoons ground cumin
2 teaspoons paprika
1 teaspoon dried oregano
¼ teaspoon cayenne pepper

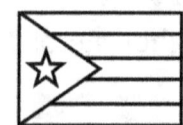

- ⅛ teaspoon ground cloves
- ⅛ teaspoon ground allspice
- ½ cup white wine
- 1½ cups tomato sauce
- 1½ cups chicken broth
- 2 bay leaves
- 2 bell peppers, sliced
- 1 poblano pepper, sliced
- ½ teaspoon smoked paprika
- 2 tablespoons capers, drained
- 1 cup pimento-stuffed green olives, sliced
- 1 teaspoon white sugar, or to taste (Optional)
- ⅓ cup chopped fresh cilantro

DIRECTIONS:

1

Cut flank steak in half across the grain. Mix salt, black pepper, and cayenne. Season both sides generously with the salt mixture.

2

Heat olive oil in a pot over high heat. Add steaks and cook until outsides are well browned, 4 to 5 minutes per side. Remove steaks to a plate.

3

Reduce heat to medium. Add red onion, garlic, and more of the salt seasoning. Cook and stir until starting to soften, 3 to 5 minutes. Stir in cumin, paprika, oregano, cayenne pepper, cloves, and allspice. Cook and stir for 1 minute. Pour in white wine, scraping up the browned bits from the bottom of the pot. Stir in tomato sauce and chicken broth.

4

Return beef and accumulated juices to the pot. Season with salt and add bay leaves. Reduce heat to low, cover, and simmer until beef is almost fork-tender, not falling apart, about 2 hours.

5

Remove pot from heat and let stew cool to room temperature, at least 45 minutes. Refrigerate, 8 hours to overnight, for best results.

6

Remove beef to a plate and set stew over medium heat. Tear beef along the grain into 1/8- to 1/4-inch-wide shreds; place back in the stew. Add bell peppers, poblanos, smoked paprika, capers, olives, and sugar. Stir together and reduce heat to medium. Simmer until peppers are soft and meat is tender, 15 to 20 minutes. Turn off heat, remove bay leaves, and stir in cilantro.

NUTRITION FACTS:

209 calories; protein 11.9g; carbohydrates 10.4g; fat 12.5g;

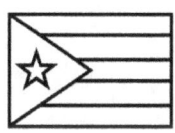

MIAMI CUBAN DIP

Prep:
15 mins
Cook:
17 mins
Total:
32 mins
Servings:
22
Yield:
2 -3/4 cups

INGREDIENTS:

1 (16 ounce) loaf Italian bread
1 cup milk
1 package Pork Gravy Mix
1 ½ cups shredded Swiss cheese, divided
5 tablespoons dill pickles, coarsely chopped, divided
¼ cup mayonnaise
1 tablespoon prepared yellow mustard
½ cup cubed ham
1 cup deli-sliced roast pork cut into bite-size pieces

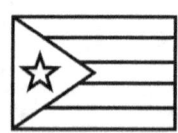

DIRECTIONS:

1

Preheat oven to 350 degrees F.

2

Place bread on baking sheet. Cut an oval on top of bread and remove bread center to make room for the dip. Tear removed bread top and bread center into bite-size pieces. Set aside for serving.

3

Whisk milk gradually into gravy mix in medium saucepan. Stirring frequently, cook over medium heat until gravy comes to a boil. Reduce heat to simmer. Stir in 1 1/4 cups of the cheese, 4 tablespoons of the pickles, mayonnaise, and mustard. Cook 2 to 3 minutes or until cheese is melted. Stir in pork and ham.

4

Spoon dip into bread. Sprinkle with remaining 1/4 cup cheese.

5

Bake 10 minutes or until cheese is melted and bread is warm. Sprinkle dip with remaining 1 tablespoon chopped pickles. Serve with bread pieces.

NUTRITION FACTS:

126 calories; protein 6.4g; carbohydrates 12.3g; fat 5.5g; cholesterol 15.1mg; sodium 291.2mg.

CUBAN PORK ROAST

Servings:
8
Yield:
8 servings

INGREDIENTS:

2 teaspoons cumin seeds
½ teaspoon whole black peppercorns
4 cloves garlic, chopped
2 teaspoons salt
1 teaspoon dried oregano
⅓ cup orange juice
⅓ cup dry sherry
3 tablespoons lemon juice
3 tablespoons fresh lime juice
2 tablespoons olive oil
4 pounds pork shoulder, trimmed and tied

DIRECTIONS:

1

Heat a small, heavy skillet over medium heat. Add the cumin seeds and peppercorns to the pan; stir constantly until fragrant and beginning to brown, about 2 minutes. Cool.

2

Using a mortar and pestle, crush toasted spices with garlic, salt, and oregano to make a paste. You can also do this in the small bowl of a food processor. Transfer to a small bowl, and stir in orange juice, lime juice, lemon juice, sherry, and olive oil.

3

Place the pork in a large resealable plastic bag. Pour citrus marinade over meat, and seal. Refrigerate for 12 to 24 hours, turning the bag over occasionally.

4

Preheat the oven to 325 degrees F (165 degrees C).

5

Transfer pork and marinade to a roasting pan, and place in the oven. Roast for about 2 1/2 hours, basting with pan juices occasionally, or until an instant read thermometer inserted in the center reads 145 degrees F (63 degrees C). Add small amounts of water to the pan if it dries out. Transfer the pork to a carving board, cover loosely with foil, and let rest for 15 minutes. Carve, and serve.

NUTRITION FACTS:

626 calories; protein 38.2g; carbohydrates 4.5g; fat 49.3g; cholesterol 161mg; sodium 796.9mg.

CUBAN SMOKED SAUSAGE WITH CHICKPEAS

Prep:
10 mins
Cook:
1 hr 10 mins
Total:
1 hr 20 mins

INGREDIENTS:

- 1 pound smoked sausage
- 2 teaspoons vegetable oil
- 1 medium onion, diced
- 2 (15.5 ounce) cans chickpeas (garbanzo beans), undrained
- 1 (4 ounce) can tomato sauce
- 3 tablespoons sherry wine or Marsala
- 2 teaspoons dried oregano
- 2 teaspoons red pepper flakes
- ½ teaspoon ground black pepper
- ½ teaspoon garlic powder
- 3 teaspoons adobo seasoning

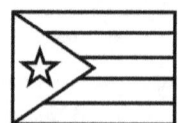

DIRECTIONS:

1

Slice sausage lengthwise, then cut into 1/4-inch slices.

2

Heat oil in a large pot over medium-high heat. Brown sausage about 5 minutes. Stir in onion; cook 5 minutes. Stir in chickpeas and juices, tomato sauce, and sherry. Season with oregano, red pepper flakes, black pepper, garlic powder, and adobo seasoning. Simmer, stirring occasionally, at least 10 minutes (1 hour or more is preferable).

NUTRITION FACTS:

510 calories; protein 24.9g; carbohydrates 40.4g; fat 27.6g; cholesterol 51.5mg;

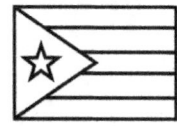

CUBAN BEANS AND RICE

Prep:
10 mins
Cook:
50 mins
Total:
60 mins
Servings:
6
Yield:
6 servings

INGREDIENTS:

1 tablespoon olive oil
1 cup chopped onion
1 green bell pepper, chopped
2 cloves garlic, minced
1 teaspoon salt
4 tablespoons tomato paste
1 (15.25 ounce) can kidney beans, drained with liquid reserved
1 cup uncooked white rice

DIRECTIONS:

1

Heat oil in a large saucepan over medium heat. Saute onion, bell pepper and garlic. When onion is translucent add salt and tomato paste. Reduce heat to low and cook 2 minutes. Stir in the beans and rice.

2

Pour the liquid from the beans into a large measuring cup and add enough water to reach a volume of 2 1/2 cups; pour into beans. Cover and cook on low for 45 to 50 minutes, or until liquid is absorbed and rice is cooked.

NUTRITION FACTS:

258 calories; protein 7.3g; carbohydrates 49.3g; fat 3.2g; cholesterol 1.6mg;

CUBAN BLACK BEANS

Prep:
15 mins
Cook:
1 hr 30 mins
Additional:
8 hrs
Total:
9 hrs 45 mins
Servings:
8

INGREDIENTS:

1 pound black beans, washed
¼ cup olive oil
1 large onion, chopped
1 medium green bell pepper, chopped
6 cloves garlic, peeled and minced
5 cups water
1 (6 ounce) can tomato paste
1 (4 ounce) jar diced pimentos, drained
1 tablespoon vinegar
2 teaspoons salt
1 teaspoon white sugar
1 teaspoon black pepper

DIRECTIONS:

1

Place beans in a large saucepan with enough water to cover, and soak 8 hours, or overnight; drain.

2

Heat oil in a medium saucepan over medium heat, and saute onion, green bell pepper, and garlic until tender.

3

Into the onion mixture, stir the drained beans, water, tomato paste, pimentos, and vinegar. Season with salt, sugar, and pepper. Bring to a boil. Cover, reduce heat, and simmer 1 1/2 hours, stirring occasionally, until beans are tender.

NUTRITION FACTS:

290 calories; protein 13.8g; carbohydrates 44g; fat 7.8g;

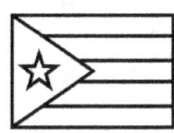

CLASSIC CUBAN MIDNIGHT

Prep:
15 mins
Cook:
8 mins
Total:
23 mins
Servings:
4
Yield:
4 sandwiches

INGREDIENTS:

4 sweet bread rolls
½ cup mayonnaise
¼ cup prepared mustard
1 pound thinly sliced cooked ham
1 pound thinly sliced fully cooked pork
1 pound sliced Swiss cheese
1 cup dill pickle slices
2 tablespoons butter, melted

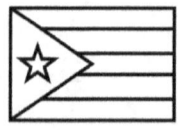

DIRECTIONS:

1

Split the sandwich rolls in half, and spread mustard and mayonnaise liberally onto the cut sides. On each sandwich, place and equal amount of Swiss cheese, ham and pork in exactly that order. Place a few pickles onto each one, and put the top of the roll onto the sandwich. Brush the tops with melted butter.

2

Press each sandwich in a sandwich press heated to medium-high heat. If a sandwich press is not available, use a large skillet over medium-high heat, and press the sandwiches down using a sturdy plate or skillet. Some indoor grills may be good for this also. Cook for 5 to 8 minutes, keeping sandwiches pressed. If using a skillet, you may want to flip them once for even browning. Slice diagonally and serve hot.

NUTRITION FACTS:

1453 calories; protein 92.1g; carbohydrates 69.1g; fat 88.4g; cholesterol 275.2mg

CUBAN GOULASH

Prep:
20 mins
Cook:
40 mins
Total:
60 mins
Servings:
6
Yield:
6 servings

INGREDIENTS:

1 tablespoon vegetable oil
1 pound boneless pork roast, cubed
1 pound onions, diced
1 pound bananas, peeled and diced
1 (16 ounce) can diced tomatoes with juice
cayenne pepper to taste
salt and ground black pepper to taste

DIRECTIONS:

1

Heat the oil in a large skillet over medium heat, and brown the pork on all sides. Mix in the onions, and cook and stir until tender.

2

Mix the bananas and tomatoes with juice into the skillet. Bring to a boil, reduce heat to medium low, and simmer 30 minutes, stirring occasionally, until pork is very tender. Season with cayenne pepper, salt, and pepper.

NUTRITION FACTS:

197 calories; protein 11g; carbohydrates 26.9g; fat 5.5g; cholesterol 26.5mg; sodium 137.9mg

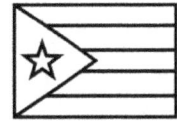

CUBAN GREEN SOUP

Prep:
1 min
Cook:
30 mins
Total:
31 mins
Servings:
8
Yield:
8 servings

INGREDIENTS:

2 ounces salt pork, diced
1 large onion, chopped
5 (15 ounce) cans navy beans, with juice
2 (10 ounce) packages frozen turnip greens with turnip pieces

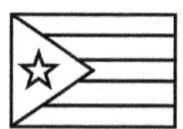

DIRECTIONS:

1

Place a stock pot or Dutch oven over medium heat. Fry the salt pork for a few minutes to release some liquid. Add onion, and saute until translucent. Stir in the navy beans and turnip greens. Bring to a boil, reduce heat to medium-low, and simmer for about 30 minutes. Serve with home made pepper vinegar and a side of cornbread for restaurant-style dining.

NUTRITION FACTS:

372 calories; protein 22.1g; carbohydrates 57.8g; fat 7g; cholesterol 6.1mg;

AMAZING CUBAN TAMALES

Prep:
1 hr 30 mins
Cook:
2 hrs 10 mins
Additional:
3 hrs
Total:
6 hrs 40 mins
Servings:
14
Yield:
28 tamales

INGREDIENTS:

¼ cup olive oil, divided
1½ pounds boneless country-style pork ribs, cut into small pieces
1 cup dry white wine, divided
2 cups water
10 cloves garlic, minced, divided
2 tablespoons tomato paste, divided
2 cubes beef bouillon
2 bay leaves

1 teaspoon ground cumin
1 teaspoon dried oregano
½ teaspoon ground black pepper
2 links Spanish chorizo sausage (such as Goya®), thinly sliced
1 yellow onion, diced
1 small green bell pepper, chopped
½ cup pimento-stuffed green olives
4 cups frozen corn, thawed
1½ cups masa harina
2 tablespoons white sugar
1 tablespoon white vinegar
1 teaspoon salt, or to taste
1 (8 ounce) package dried corn husks, soaked in warm water
kitchen twine, cut into 12-inch lengths

DIRECTIONS:

1

Heat 2 tablespoons olive oil in large saucepan or Dutch oven over medium-high heat. Cook and stir pork in hot oil until lightly browned, 5 to 7 minutes.

2

Pour 1/2 cup white wine into saucepan and bring to a boil while scraping the browned bits of food off of the bottom of the pan with a wooden spoon.

3

Stir 2 cups water, 5 cloves garlic, 1 tablespoon tomato paste, 1 beef bouillon cube, bay leaves, cumin, oregano, and black pepper to pork mixture. Bring mixture to a boil, reduce heat to low, partially cover the saucepan with a lid, and simmer until pork is very tender, 1 to 2 hours. Transfer pork to a bowl and reserve cooking liquid.

4

Heat remaining olive oil in a deep pot over medium-high heat. Cook and stir chorizo and cooked pork in hot oil until lightly browned, 3 to 5 minutes.

5

Stir onion, green pepper, and remaining minced garlic into chorizo mixture; saute until vegetables soften and onion is translucent, about 5 minutes. Add remaining white wine, olives, 1 tablespoon tomato paste, and remaining bouillon cube; cook, stirring frequently, until flavors combine, about 5 minutes more.

6

Pulse corn and 1 1/2 cups reserved pork broth together in a blender or food processor until mixture has a thick and chunky consistency. Stir corn mixture into pork-chorizo mixture.

7

Reduce heat to medium and stir masa harina, sugar, vinegar, and salt into pork mixture; cook, stirring occasionally, until mixture has a hearty cornmeal porridge-consistency. Season with salt and remove from heat.

8

Make a pocket out of one corn husk and fill 3/4 full with pork mixture, leaving a top flap. Wrap another husk around the filled pocket. Fold top flap over the pocket. Tie twine length- and width-wise around the tamale several times so that packet is secure, but has room for filling to expand during cooking. Repeat with remaining husks and filling.

9

Fill a pot with 2-inches of water; bring to a simmer. Place tamales upright in simmering water, cover the pot, and cook, adding water as necessary, until filling is hot and set, about 40 minutes. Cool tamales until completely set, at least 3 hours.

NUTRITION FACTS:

284 calories; protein 11.4g; carbohydrates 24g; fat 15.4g; cholesterol 33.2mg; sodium 603.9mg.

TAMPA CUBAN HAND PIES

Prep:
15 mins
Cook:
25 mins
Additional:
5 mins
Total:
45 mins
Servings:
4
Yield:
4 hand pies

INGREDIENTS:

- 1 (8 ounce) can crescent dough sheet
- 2 tablespoons yellow mustard
- ¼ pound sliced ham
- ¼ pound sliced cooked pork loin
- ¼ pound sliced Genoa salami
- 4 slices Swiss cheese, cut to fit
- 8 dill pickle chips, dried with a paper towel
- 1 egg
- 1 tablespoon milk

DIRECTIONS:

1
Preheat the oven to 375 degrees F (190 degrees C). Line a baking sheet with parchment paper.

2
Remove dough from the can and roll out into a 9x16-inch rectangle. Cut into 4 equal rectangles.

3
Place 1 rectangle horizontally on a work surface. Brush mustard over the surface, leaving a 1/2-inch border. Arrange ham, pork, salami, Swiss cheese, and 2 pickle chips, in that order, on the left side of the rectangle. Leave the border and right side of the dough exposed.

4
Whisk egg and milk together to make an egg wash. Brush around the border. Fold the right side over the filling and press to seal; crimp the edges with a fork. Cut a few small slits in the top of the hand pie to vent. Brush some egg wash over the top.

5
Repeat with remaining dough, mustard, filling, and egg wash. Arrange hand pies on the prepared baking sheet.

6
Bake in the preheated oven until crisp and golden brown, 22 to 25 minutes. Cover with foil if starting to brown too quickly. Remove pies to a rack to cool for 5 minutes

NUTRITION FACTS:

574 calories; protein 32.1g; carbohydrates 25.1g; fat 37.1g;

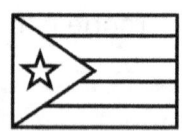

CUBAN-STYLE YELLOW RICE

Prep:
10 mins
Cook:
20 mins
Total:
30 mins
Servings:
24
Yield:
12 cups

INGREDIENTS:

4 cups long grain rice
8 cups water
1 small onion, minced
2 teaspoons salt
⅛ teaspoon annatto powder
⅛ teaspoon paprika
black pepper to taste
1 cup frozen peas, thawed
1 (4 ounce) jar sliced pimento peppers, for garnish

DIRECTIONS:

1

Place the rice in a sieve and rinse under cold water until the water runs clear. Shake sieve to remove excess water from rice.

2

Place rice in a large saucepan with a tightly fitting lid and add water. Stir in the onion, salt, annatto powder, paprika, and pepper. Bring the mixture to a boil over medium-high heat. Reduce heat to low, cover pan, and simmer. After cooking for 10 minutes, gently stir the peas into the rice. Cook until all the water is evaporated and the rice is tender, 15 to 20 minutes longer. Serve garnished with pimento slices.

NUTRITION FACTS:

120 calories; protein 2.6g; carbohydrates 26.1g; fat 0.2g; sodium 205.6mg.

GRILLED TURKEY CUBAN SANDWICHES

Prep:
15 mins
Cook:
2 hrs
Total:
2 hrs 15 mins

INGREDIENTS:

Non-stick cooking spray
1 (3 pound) Butterball® Boneless Breast of Turkey Roast, thawed
2 cloves garlic, peeled, sliced
1 tablespoon canola oil
1 tablespoon ground cumin
2 teaspoons salt
1 teaspoon coarsely ground black pepper
2 loaves Cuban, French or Italian bread (15 inches long)
¼ cup honey mustard
½ pound smoked ham
½ pound sliced Swiss cheese
12 sandwich-style dill pickle slices

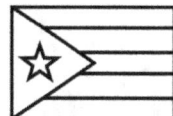

DIRECTIONS:

1

Spray cold grate of outdoor gas grill with cooking spray. Prepare grill for medium indirect heat.

2

Remove turkey from package. Dry with paper towels. Discard gravy packet or refrigerate for another use (within 2 - 3 days). Lift string netting and shift position on roast for easier removal after cooking. Cut small slits, at least 1 inch apart, over entire surface of turkey. Insert 1 garlic slice into each slit. Brush turkey with oil.

3

Combine cumin, salt and pepper. Sprinkle over turkey.

4

Place turkey on grill grate over drip pan. Cover grill with lid. Grill 1 1/4 to 1-3/4 hours, or until meat thermometer reaches 170 degrees F when inserted into center of roast. Remove from grill. Let stand 10 minutes.

5

Remove string netting. Cut half of the turkey into six 1/8-inch-thick slices. Set aside. Refrigerate unsliced turkey for another use.

6

Cut each bread loaf lengthwise in half. Then, cut each into 3 pieces (for 6 sandwiches). Spread the bottom half of each section with 2 teaspoons mustard. Top with the sliced turkey, ham, cheese and pickles. Cover with tops of bread loaves. Press sandwiches with hands to flatten. Tightly wrap individually in aluminum foil.

7

Place wrapped sandwiches on grill grate. Top each with heavy iron skillet or brick. Grill 3 to 5 minutes on each side, or until heated through.

8

Serve sandwiches warm, wrapped in aluminum foil.

NUTRITION FACTS:

1066 calories; protein 91.6g; carbohydrates 95.1g; fat 34.4g; cholesterol 202.4mg; sodium 2711.5mg

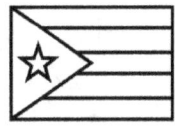

CUBAN MARINATED STEAK

Prep:
15 mins
Cook:
15 mins
Additional:
35 mins
Total:
65 mins
Servings:
4
Yield:
4 servings

INGREDIENTS:

- ½ teaspoon cumin seeds
- ¼ cup orange juice
- 2 tablespoons vegetable oil
- 2 tablespoons Montreal-style steak seasoning
- 2¼ teaspoons lime juice
- 1½ teaspoons dried oregano
- 1½ pounds beef rib-eye steaks

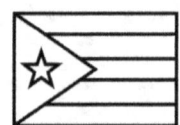

DIRECTIONS:

1

Place cumin seeds into a small skillet over medium heat; stir constantly until seeds turn dark brown and smell toasted, about 1 minute. Immediately pour seeds into a bowl to stop the cooking. Mix cumin seeds with orange juice, vegetable oil, steak seasoning, lime juice, and oregano in a bowl.

2

Place steaks into a large resealable plastic bag, pour orange juice marinade over the meat, and squeeze out air. Seal bag and turn it over several times to coat meat with marinade. Refrigerate at least 30 minutes, or longer for extra flavor.

3

Preheat an outdoor grill for medium-high heat and lightly oil the grate.

4

Remove steaks from marinade, shaking off any excess. Discard used marinade. Grill steaks on the preheated grill until seared on the outsides and still slightly pink in the centers, 6 to 8 minutes per side. An instant-read meat thermometer inserted sideways into the center of the thickest steak should read 145 degrees F (65 degrees C). Let steaks rest for 3 minutes before slicing.

NUTRITION FACTS:

245 calories; protein 21.2g; carbohydrates 3.9g; fat 15.8g; cholesterol 59.4mg;

FRITAS CUBANAS

Prep:
30 mins
Cook:
10 mins
Total:
40 mins

INGREDIENTS:

2 yellow onions, quartered
2 (4 ounce) links chorizo sausage, casings removed
1 green bell pepper, quartered and seeded
6 cloves clove garlic
1 pound lean ground beef
1 pound ground pork
1 cup Italian-style bread crumbs
2 eggs, beaten
2 tablespoons ketchup
1 dash ground cumin
sea salt to taste
freshly ground black pepper
1 tablespoon vegetable oil, or as needed
12 hamburger buns, split
1 (9 ounce) can shoestring potatoes

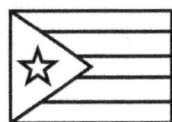

DIRECTIONS:

1

Place yellow onions, chorizo, green bell pepper, and garlic in a food processor; pulse until minced.

2

Transfer onion mixture to a large bowl. Add ground beef, ground pork, bread crumbs, eggs, ketchup, cumin, salt, and black pepper; mix with your hands until well-blended.

3

Form mixture into 12 patties.

4

Heat oil in a large skillet over medium heat. Cook patties in batches until browned and medium well done, about 5 minutes per side.

5

Serve cooked patties on hamburger buns topped with shoestring potatoes.

NUTRITION FACTS:

558 calories; protein 25.1g; carbohydrates 44.8g; fat 30g; cholesterol 91mg; sodium 720.7mg.

RABBIT FRICASSEE CUBAN-STYLE

Prep:
30 mins
Cook:
45 mins
Total:
75 mins
Servings:
6
Yield:
6 servings

INGREDIENTS:

1 (3 pound) rabbit, cleaned and cut into pieces
2 ½ cups water
1 large onion, chopped
3 cloves garlic, chopped
1 green bell pepper, chopped
¼ teaspoon saffron powder
1 teaspoon ground cumin
1 teaspoon salt, or to taste
1 teaspoon black pepper
2 tablespoons fresh lemon juice
1 bay leaf

1 (8 ounce) can tomato sauce
1 pound potatoes, peeled and quartered
¼ cup dry white wine
¼ cup capers, drained
1 cup raisins
¼ cup chopped green olives
¼ cup olive oil
1 (10 ounce) can baby peas, drained

DIRECTIONS:

1

Place the rabbit pieces in a deep skillet or Dutch oven over medium heat along with the onion, garlic, and green pepper. Season with saffron, cumin, salt, pepper, lemon juice and the bay leaf. Pour the water over all. Bring to a boil, then simmer for 20 minutes.

2

Add the potatoes, and cook for about 20 more minutes, until tender. Add the raisins, capers, white wine, tomato sauce, olives and olive oil. Simmer for about 5 more minutes. Finally, stir in the peas and remove from the heat.

NUTRITION FACTS:

578 calories; protein 47.9g; carbohydrates 46g; fat 22.3g; cholesterol 122.1mg; sodium 1045.3mg

CUBAN-STYLE MOJO SHRIMP

Prep:
25 mins
Cook:
10 mins
Additional:
15 mins
Total:
50 mins
Servings:
4
Yield:
4 servings

INGREDIENTS:

½ cup lime juice
¼ cup orange juice
¼ cup grapefruit juice
¼ cup lemon juice
¼ cup vinegar
¼ cup extra-virgin olive oil
5 cloves garlic, peeled and chopped
½ teaspoon dried Mexican oregano
¼ teaspoon red pepper flakes, or to taste

¼ teaspoon ground cumin
1 pinch salt and ground black pepper to taste
1 pound fresh shrimp - peeled, deveined, and tails removed
2 tablespoons chopped fresh cilantro (Optional)

DIRECTIONS:

1

Pour lime, orange, grapefruit, and lemon juices into a blender or food processor. Add vinegar, oil, garlic, Mexican oregano, red pepper flakes, and cumin. Pulse several times, then blend until the garlic pieces disappear, about 1 minute. Season with salt and pepper and pulse one more time.

2

Pour marinade into a 1-gallon resealable bag and add shrimp. Squeeze most of the air out of the bag and seal. Refrigerate for 15 minutes, with the shrimp inside the bag in a single layer. Drain and reserve marinade.

3

Heat a nonstick skillet over medium heat and cook shrimp in a single layer, 1 to 1 1/2 minutes per side. Shrimp are done when they are opaque, pink and white, and curled into a "C" shape. Remove shrimp from the skillet and set aside.

4

Pour reserved marinade into the same skillet and bring to a boil. Boil until marinade is reduced to about 2/3 cup, about 6 minutes. Pour into a small serving pitcher or sauce boat.

5

Serve shrimp with sauce on the side as a dipping sauce, or toss shrimp in the sauce. Garnish with fresh cilantro.

NUTRITION FACTS:

372 calories; protein 19.6g; carbohydrates 18.6g; fat 25g; cholesterol 156.6mg; sodium 345.4mg.

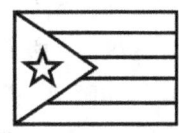

SEA BASS CUBAN STYLE

Prep:
20 mins
Cook:
25 mins
Total:
45 mins
Servings:
4
Yield:
4 servings

INGREDIENTS:

2 tablespoons extra virgin olive oil
1 ½ cups thinly sliced white onions
2 tablespoons minced garlic
4 cups seeded, chopped plum tomatoes
1 ½ cups dry white wine
⅔ cup sliced stuffed green olives
¼ cup drained capers
⅛ teaspoon red pepper flakes
4 (6 ounce) fillets sea bass
2 tablespoons butter
¼ cup chopped fresh cilantro

DIRECTIONS:

1

Heat oil in a large skillet over medium heat. Saute onions until soft. Stir in garlic, and saute about 1 minute. Add tomatoes, and cook until they begin to soften. Stir in wine, olives, capers, and red pepper flakes. Heat to a simmer.

2

Place sea bass into sauce. Cover, and gently simmer for 10 to 12 minutes, or until fish flakes easily with a fork. Transfer fish to a serving plate, and keep warm.

3

Increase the heat, and add butter to sauce. Simmer until the sauce thickens. Stir in cilantro. Serve sauce over fish.

NUTRITION FACTS:

444 calories; protein 34.2g; carbohydrates 17.4g; fat 19.4g;

AMAZING LOMO DE RES, CUBAN-STYLE RIB-EYE STEAKS

Prep:
10 mins
Cook:
10 mins
Additional:
30 mins
Total:
50 mins
Servings:
4

INGREDIENTS:

- 1 tablespoon garlic powder
- 1 tablespoon onion powder
- 1 tablespoon meat tenderizer
- 1 tablespoon seasoning salt
- 2 pounds rib-eye steak, 1/4 inch thick
- 1 onion, sliced
- 1 (12 ounce) bottle beer
- 1¼ cups fresh lime juice

DIRECTIONS:

1

Mix together the garlic powder, onion powder, meat tenderizer, and seasoning salt in a small bowl. Rub the seasoning blend into both sides of the steaks.

2

Arrange 1/4 of the sliced onions in the bottom of a 9x13 inch pan, lay steaks across the onions, top with more onions and pour 1/4 cup of lime juice and 1/4 of the bottle of beer over the top; repeat these layers until you run out of steaks, pouring all remaining lime juice and beer over the top. Cover and refrigerate for 30 to 40 minutes. Do not marinate the steaks for longer than an hour, because the acid from the lime juice in the marinade will begin to cook the meat.

3

Preheat an outdoor grill for medium-high heat and lightly oil grate. Place steaks on the grill and discard the marinade.

4

Grill the steaks to your desired degree of doneness, or about 2 minutes per side for well done. Remove from the grill and allow to rest for 5 minutes before slicing and serving with warm tortillas.

NUTRITION FACTS:

389 calories; protein 27.9g; carbohydrates 16.2g; fat 21.3g; cholesterol 81.2mg; sodium 1103.3mg.

BAKED CUBAN CHICKEN

Prep:
15 mins
Cook:
50 mins
Additional:
1 hr
Total:
1 hr 65 mins
Servings:
6
Yield:
6 servings

INGREDIENTS:

2 (8 ounce) bone-in chicken breasts, cut in half
2 bone-in chicken thighs
2 chicken drumsticks
1 onion, chopped
¾ cup lemon juice
¼ cup Worcestershire sauce
1 ½ tablespoons minced garlic
¾ teaspoon ground allspice
½ teaspoon onion powder

¼ teaspoon ground cumin
¼ teaspoon red pepper flakes
1 pinch salt and ground black pepper to taste
cooking spray
1 tablespoon vegetable oil

DIRECTIONS:

1

Place chicken pieces in a large bowl. Add onion, lemon juice, Worcestershire sauce, garlic, allspice, onion powder, cumin, red pepper flakes, salt, and pepper. Stir thoroughly. Cover and refrigerate for 1 hour, or overnight.

2

Preheat the oven to 375 degrees F (190 degrees C). Lightly grease a 9x13-inch baking dish with cooking spray.

3

Heat oil in a large skillet. Add chicken pieces, reserving marinade in the bowl. Pan-fry chicken until browned, about 5 minutes per side. Transfer to the prepared baking dish. Pour reserved marinade on top.

4

Bake in the preheated oven until juices run clear, about 40 minutes.

NUTRITION FACTS:

270 calories; protein 28.4g; carbohydrates 9.5g; fat 12.9g; cholesterol 87.2mg; sodium 217.7mg.

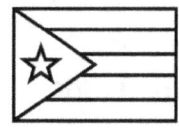

CUBAN-STYLE PORK AND SWEET POTATOES

Prep:
15 mins
Cook:
6 hrs
Total:
6 hrs 15 mins
Servings:
6
Yield:
6 servings

INGREDIENTS:

1½ pounds sweet potatoes, cut into 1/2-inch cubes
1 pound pork, cut into 1-inch squares
1 (15 ounce) can diced tomatoes with green chile peppers
¼ cup orange juice
1½ tablespoons lime juice
2 cloves garlic, pressed
¼ teaspoon ground cumin
¼ teaspoon salt
¼ teaspoon ground black pepper

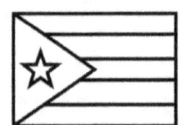

¼ cup chopped fresh cilantro, or to taste

DIRECTIONS:

1

Mix sweet potatoes, pork, diced tomatoes with green chile peppers, orange juice, lime juice, garlic, cumin, salt, and black pepper together in a slow cooker.

2

Cook on Low for 6 hours. Garnish with cilantro.

NUTRITION FACTS:

266 calories; protein 17.4g; carbohydrates 27.3g; fat 9.7g; cholesterol 47.6mg; sodium 483.2mg.

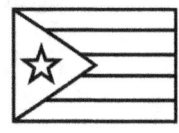

CHICKEN FRIED STEAK CUBAN STYLE

Prep:
15 mins
Cook:
30 mins
Total:
45 mins
Servings:
4
Yield:
4 steaks

INGREDIENTS:

4 (4 ounce) cube steaks
2 eggs
3 cups dry bread crumbs
1 tablespoon dried oregano
1 teaspoon ground cumin
salt and pepper to taste
1 lemon, sliced
2 cups vegetable oil for frying

DIRECTIONS:

1

In a shallow dish, combine the breadcrumbs with the oregano, cumin, and salt and pepper. Beat eggs in another shallow dish. Dip each steak in beaten eggs, and then in the breadcrumb mixture. Make sure to cover each steak well with the breadcrumb mixture.

2

In a large, deep skillet, heat 1inch oil over medium high heat.

3

Place the steaks in the oil when it's hot (so that the breading will not stick to the pan). Cook steaks, turning once, until brown for well done and golden brown for medium. Serve with lemon slices.

NUTRITION FACTS:

577 calories; protein 28.4g; carbohydrates 62.3g; fat 24g;

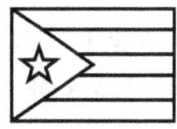

TURKEY PICADILLO

Prep:
15 mins
Cook:
25 mins
Total:
40 mins

INGREDIENTS:

1 tablespoon olive oil
1 pound ground turkey
1 ½ teaspoons olive oil
1 large yellow onion, chopped
1 green bell pepper, chopped
4 cloves garlic, minced
2 bay leaves
½ cup white wine
1 (8 ounce) can tomato sauce
⅓ cup chopped green olives
⅓ cup raisins
½ cup canned black beans
1 tablespoon olive brine
1 tablespoon capers
2 teaspoons cayenne pepper, or to taste
2 teaspoons ground cumin

DIRECTIONS:

1

Heat 1 tablespoon olive oil in a large skillet over medium-high heat and stir in the ground turkey. Cook and stir until the turkey is crumbly, evenly browned, and no longer pink. Remove the turkey and drain and discard any excess grease.

2

Heat 1 1/2 teaspoons olive oil in the skillet over medium heat. Add the onions, bell pepper, garlic, and bay leaves; cook and stir until the onion has softened and turned translucent, about 5 minutes. Stir in the cooked turkey, wine, tomato sauce, olives, raisins, black beans, olive brine, capers, cayenne, and cumin. Simmer about 15 minutes.

NUTRITION FACTS:

246 calories; protein 17.9g; carbohydrates 17.9g; fat 10.8g; cholesterol 55.8mg; sodium 589.8mg.

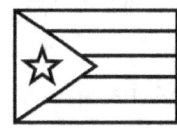

SPICY CUBAN MOJO CHICKEN WITH MANGO-AVOCADO SALSA

Prep:
40 mins
Cook:
25 mins
Additional:
2 hrs 30 mins
Total:
2 hrs 95 mins
Servings:
4
Yield:
4 servings

INGREDIENTS:

1 teaspoon cumin seed
3 cloves garlic, chopped
1 fresh red chile pepper, chopped
¼ teaspoon salt
2 tablespoons olive oil

5 teaspoons orange juice
5 teaspoons lemon juice
2 (8 ounce) boneless, skinless chicken breast halves
2 tablespoons olive oil
½ cup orange juice
1 teaspoon lime zest
1 teaspoon honey
1 teaspoon sweet soy sauce
¼ cup cold, unsalted butter, cut into pieces
½ cup diced mango
½ avocado
chopped fresh cilantro to taste
chopped fresh parsley to taste

DIRECTIONS:

1

Toast the cumin seeds in a dry skillet over medium-high heat until fragrant, about 2 minutes. Place the cumin seeds, garlic, chile pepper, salt, olive oil, orange juice, and lemon juice into the bowl of a blender; grind to a coarse paste. Toss the chicken with the marinade, then place into the refrigerator, and allow to marinate for about 2 1/2 hours.

2

Preheat oven to 350 degrees F (175 degrees C).

3

Heat a skillet over medium-high heat. Cook the chicken for 2 to 3 minutes on each side until browned. Place into the oven, and cook until the juices run clear, about 8 minutes. When the chicken is done, remove, cover with foil, and allow to rest for 3 to 5 minutes.

4

While the chicken is in the oven, whisk together the olive oil, orange juice, lime zest, honey, and soy sauce in a skillet over medium-high heat. Simmer until the orange juice has reduced to 1/3 of original volume and is beginning to get thick and syrupy. Once thick, remove from heat, and whisk in the butter pieces one at a time until melted; set aside.

5

To serve, place chicken on the plate and sprinkle with mango and avocado. Drizzle with the sauce, and garnish with cilantro and parsley.

NUTRITION FACTS:

441 calories; protein 25.2g; carbohydrates 15.4g; fat 31.7g; cholesterol 95.1mg; sodium 364.3mg

CUBAN BEEF AND ZUCCHINI KEBABS WITH MOJO SAUCE

Prep:
25 mins
Cook:
10 mins
Total:
35 mins
Servings:
4

INGREDIENTS:

SAUCE:

4 cloves garlic, coarsely chopped
½ teaspoon salt
½ cup fresh orange juice
3 tablespoons fresh lime juice

2 tablespoons olive oil
½ teaspoon cumin
½ teaspoon dried oregano

SKEWERS:

1 (16 ounce) sirloin steak (1 inch thick), cut into 1 1/4-inch pieces
8 (12-inch) wooden skewers, soaked in water 30 minutes
½ teaspoon salt
¼ teaspoon black pepper
2 (10 ounce) zucchini, cut on a long diagonal into 1/2-inch-thick slices
2 tablespoons olive oil

DIRECTIONS:

1

Mash garlic to a paste with salt using a mortar and pestle or flat side of a large knife, then whisk together with orange juice, lime juice, olive oil, cumin and oregano in a bowl.

2

Preheat an outdoor grill to medium-high heat (375 degrees F to 450 degrees F).

3

Thread beef on 4 skewers, leaving a little space between each piece. Put skewers on a baking sheet and sprinkle all over with salt and pepper. Thread zucchini onto 4 skewers so slices can grill cut sides down, then transfer to baking sheet.
Lightly brush beef and zucchini all over with oil.

4

Lightly oil grate and grill beef, covered with lid, turning once, about 4 minutes total for medium rare. Transfer to a serving platter and cover with foil to keep warm.

5

Lightly oil grate again and grill zucchini, covered with lid, turning once, until grill marks appear and zucchini is just tender, 4 to 5 minutes total. Transfer skewers to a serving platter. Drizzle beef and zucchini with about half of sauce, and serve remaining sauce on the side.

NUTRITION FACTS:

308 calories; protein 22g; carbohydrates 10.3g; fat 20.4g; cholesterol 49.1mg; sodium 638.4mg.

CARNE CON PAPAS

Prep:
15 mins
Cook:
1 hr
Total:
1 hr 15 mins

INGREDIENTS:

½ green bell pepper, seeded and chopped
½ small white onion, chopped
3 cloves garlic, crushed
¼ teaspoon ground cumin
¼ teaspoon salt, divided
⅛ cup olive oil
1 tablespoon olive oil
2 tablespoons achiote powder
1 teaspoon ground cumin
2 (8 ounce) cans tomato sauce
2 pounds beef stew meat, cut into 1 inch cubes
2 white potatoes
1 cup white wine
4 cups water
6 cubes beef bouillon

DIRECTIONS:

1

In a blender, combine green pepper, onion, garlic, 1/4 teaspoon cumin and salt. Pulse, while pouring 1/8 cup olive oil through top of blender. Blend until smooth; set aside.

2

Heat 1 tablespoon olive oil in pressure cooker on medium heat. Saute green pepper mixture for 1 minute, then stir in achiote powder and 1 teaspoon cumin. Cook for 1 minute, then stir in tomato sauce. Return to a simmer, then add beef; let simmer for 5 minutes. Stir in potatoes, then pour in wine and water. Drop in the bouillon cubes. Bring to a boil, and cook for 1 minute; add water, if necessary, to cover.

3

Cover with lid of pressure cooker. Following manufacturer's directions, cook under 15 pound pressure for about 30 to 45 minutes.

NUTRITION FACTS:

612 calories; protein 44.5g; carbohydrates 20.4g; fat 35.3g; cholesterol 131.7mg; sodium 1463.5mg.

ARROZ CON LECHE

Prep:
10 mins
Cook:
40 mins
Total:
50 mins
Servings:
10
Yield:
10 servings

INGREDIENTS:

2 ¼ cups water
1 ½ cups short grain rice
1 (1/4 inch x 3 inch) strip lime peel
½ cup water
1 cinnamon stick
2 tablespoons anise seed, crushed
1 (12 ounce) can evaporated milk
1 (14 ounce) can condensed milk
1 tablespoon vanilla extract
¼ teaspoon salt
¾ cup raisins (Optional)

DIRECTIONS:

1

Combine 2 1/4 cups of water, rice, and lime peel in a saucepan. Bring to a boil over medium-high heat, then reduce heat to medium-low, cover, and simmer for 20 minutes until the rice is tender.

2

While the rice is cooking, combine 1/2 cup of water, the cinnamon stick, and anise in another saucepan over medium-high heat. Bring mixture to a low boil for 3 minutes, then remove saucepan from stove. Strain flavored water into a bowl and set aside, discarding cinnamon stick and anise pieces.

3

After rice has simmered for 20 minutes, carefully remove the lime peel with a slotted spoon, and over low heat, gradually stir evaporated milk and condensed milk into the rice. Mix in the cinnamon and anise-flavored water, vanilla, and salt. Add raisins, if desired. Continue to stir until the mixture thickens, about 7 to 10 minutes.

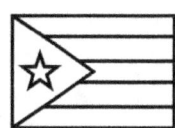

4

If the pudding is too watery after 10 minutes, turn up heat to medium-low and stir continuously. When pudding reaches desired consistency, remove from heat and pour into individual dishes, or a large bowl. Store in the refrigerator until ready to serve.

NUTRITION FACTS:

325 calories; protein 8g; carbohydrates 59.4g; fat 6.4g; cholesterol 23.2mg; sodium 148mg.

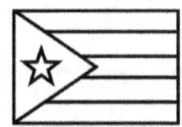

www.ingramcontent.com/pod-product-compliance
Lightning Source LLC
Chambersburg PA
CBHW070930080526
44589CB00013B/1462